AMERICAN ENGLISH
ENGLISH AMERICAN

E J Perkins

Illustration Anthony James

GW00356851

A DOMINO BOOK

Domino Books (Wales) Ltd
P O Box 32, Swansea SA1 1FN
Tel. 01792 459378 Fax. 01792 466337
www.dominobooks.co.uk
e-mail sales@dominobooks.co.uk

ISBN 185772 131 4

A Note on the Author
Joan Perkins hails from Swansea, South Wales and was a senior science teacher and principal of a girls'
public school for many years. She also worked at an American Baptist Mission School and became
interested in the nuances of American versus British English. This glossary was compiled during this
time. Subsequently, she completed a master's degree in English Linguistics at the University of Wales,
Cardiff investigating in particular, the life and career of the famous linguist, Harold Palmer.
Mrs Perkins has a son, now a medical consultant.

The Artist
Anthony James trained as an illustrator and graphic designer. He now works as a freelance artist.

PREFACE

Today, the means of communication have multiplied and peoples all over the world can 'talk' to one another by radio, television, phone, fax, satellite, the internet …The understanding of languages from other countries has never been more important. But English is the lingua franca. Language, however, never stays still. Oscar Wilde asserted that *the English have really everything in common with the Americans except the language.* To some extent, this is true today.

The two languages, American English and British English, are coming closer together. Words like, *blue-colla*r and *kickback* have become common on both sides of the Atlantic. More and more words that were exclusively American are now used by the British. Similarly, Americans adopt and adapt new British words. There are still many words which have different meanings in the two countries (false cognates). For example, *bathe* for an American means *to have a bath* while someone in Britain expects *to take a swim; bill* means *paper money* for an American such as a ten dollar bill while to the British it means *an account rendered.* Then there are those words that are foreign to one side or the other such as : American - *rinky dink, schmaltz, skillet,* British - *agony aunt, lodger and thingamajig.* Some of the differences may result in amusing confusion. For example, an American asking to wash up would be surprised to be given a bowl of dirty crockery when what he wanted was to improve his personal hygiene - a wash and brush up!

This short glossary has been written to help with the many misinterpretations that may arise when Americans visit Britain or when the British visit the USA. I hope you enjoy it and find it fun.

EJP

February, 1997

All I wanted was to wash up!

CONTENTS

Put the bag in the trunk.

AMERICAN - ENGLISH

Ask the drummer about the prices.

A

Acey-deucy	Vague
Adhesive tape	Sticking plaster
Aerosol bomb	Insecticide spray
Alligator pear	Avocado
American plan	Hotel rate including meals
Angel cake	Light, fluffy, plain cake
Annie Oakley	Free ticket to a show or an event *Named after the markswoman - these tickets sometimes have a hole in them like a bullet hole.*
Ante	Stake or wager To **ante up** - put down one's stake. **Penny ante** - cheap, small time.
Antsy	Jittery, restless - ants in his pants
Apartment	Flat
Apartment hotel	Service flats
Apartment building	Block of flats
Ape - to go ape	Very excited or angry
Apple pie order (in)	In good order, ship shape
Apple polisher	Flatterer - from the custom of taking an apple for the teacher
Ascot	Cravat, scarf worn instead of a tie
Ash can	Dustbin used for refuse
Assignment	Homework

9

B

Baby buggy/carriage	Carry cot, pram
Backlog	Surplus work/orders - a satisfactory situation
Back-up lights	Reversing lights on a car
Bad-mouth	To criticize *(to slag off)*
Bag job	Burglary by police or officials
Bag lady	Homeless woman who carries her goods in a bag
Bag - man	Collector for an illegal organization
Bags	Suitcases
Ballsy	Tough
Barkeep	Barman, bartender
Barnstorm	To tour with a theatrical group/to tour rural areas as part of a political campaign
Barrel along	To travel at speed
Baseboard	Skirting board
Bathe	To bath (**not swim,** although Americans use the term, bathing suit)
Bathing }	
Bathrobe	Dressing gown
Bawl out	To reprimand, to tell off
Bay window	A paunch, fat stomach
Bazoom	Breasts
Bellhop	Bellboy/page boy/porter
Bills	Currency e.g a dollar bill

Billfold	Wallet/notecase
Billy	Truncheon
Bird Dog	Retriever, gun dog
Biscuit	Small cake like a scone
Bleachers	Cheap, open air stands in a sports stadium
Blooper	Error/bloomer
Blotter	Official daily record, especially at a police station
Bluebook	Book recording the names of important families
Bluejacket	US Naval rating
Blue laws	Strict laws curbing drink, Sunday entertainment, sex …
Bobby pin	Hair grip, hairpin
Bobby sox	Ankle length socks (Bobby soxers were teenagers)
Boiled shirt	Stiff dress shirt/evening shirt
Boner	Mistake
Boob tube	Television
Boot camp	Basic training camp for the US Navy or Marines
Booth (telephone)	Kiosk
Brakeman	Train guard
Broad	Woman
Broil	Grill
Buck	A dollar

Buddy	Pal or mate
Buffalo	To persuade, confuse someone for gain
Bug	Insect/to annoy/irritate
Bullhorn	Megaphone
Bummer	A failure, unsuccessful person
Bureau	Chest of drawers
Bus boy	Apprentice waiter
Business suit	Lounge suit
Butt	Cigarette
	Bottom/bum
Buzz	Telephone call
	Under the influence of drink or drugs

C

Cabana	Beach hut
Caddy	Shopping trolley
Call-in	Phone-in
Can	Sacked, to shut off, to preserve food
Candy store/apple	Sweet shop, toffee apple
Caravan	Convoy
Centennial	Centenary
Chaps	Leather leggings worn when riding a horse.

Check	Bill for food or drink
	Cheque
Checkers	Game of draughts/draughts
Checking account	Current bank account
Check room	Left luggage office
Chintzy	Cheap, of little value
Chips (potato)	Crisps
Closet	Cupboard, wardrobe
Clothes pin	Clothes peg
Club soda	Soda water
Clunker	Old, decrepit car, a banger
Cockamany/cockamannie	Ridiculous, incredible
Comer	Someone who is expected to do well
Comforter	Quilt, eiderdown
Comfort station	Public convenience, rest room
Commuter ticket	Season ticket
Concert master	Leader of an orchestra or band
Condominium/condo	Owner-occupied flat
Conductor	Guard - train
Confectioners' sugar	Icing sugar
Cookie	Biscuit (sweet)
Cookie sheet	Baking tray

Cook in	Self catering at a camp site or holiday location
Copy-reader	Sub-editor
Corn	Maize
Corned beef	Salt beef
Cornstarch	Corn flour
Cot	Camp bed
Cotton	Cotton wool
Cotton candy	Candy floss
Cracker	Biscuit (unsweetened)
Crackerjack	Superior, excellent
Crazy bone	Funny bone
Cross walk	Pedestrian crossing
Cruller	A small cake, ring doughnut
Cuffs (pants)	Turn-ups (trousers)
Cured ham	Gammon
Custom made	Bespoke/made to measure

D

Dander	Temper/anger
Dandy	Good, excellent
Datebook	Pocket or desk diary, appointment book (not journal)
Davenport	Large sofa

Deacon's bench	Wooden seat for two people
Deck	Pack of cards, floor
Deck shoes	Plimsolls with thick crepe soles
Derby	Bowler hat
Desk clerk	Receptionist
Diaper	Nappy
Dick	Detective
Diner	Inexpensive restaurant
Dirt road	Unpaved road
Dishpan	Washing-up bowl *(Dishpan hands* are rough usually because of the use of cheap soaps.)
Divided Highway	Dual carriageway
Down town	City centre
Draft	Conscription
Drapes	Opaque curtains (not net curtains)
Dresser	Chest of drawers
Druggist	Chemist
Drugstore/pharmacy	Chemist's shop
Drummer	Commercial traveller
Drygoods, store	Draper
Duded-up	All dressed up
Duplex	Semi-detached

E

Eavestrough	Guttering
Editorial	Leading article in a newspaper
Eggnog	Egg flip
Eggplant	Aubergine
Elevator	Lift, or place for storing grain - silo
Enjoin	To forbid (opposite of English meaning)
Eraser	Rubber
Estate tax	Death duties
Expressway	Motorway
Eyeball	To be able to see someone *I've got him eyeballed.*

F

Fall	Autumn
Faucet	Tap
Fender	Wing or mudguard of a car
Field hockey	Hockey (**Hockey** means ice hockey.)
Filling station	Petrol station
Firecracker	Firework
Fire plug	Fire hydrant
First floor	Ground floor
Fish story	Untrue or exaggerated account
Flapjack	Pancake
Flashlight	Torch

Formula	Baby's liquid feed
Freeway	Motorway
French fries	Chips
Fresh paint	Wet paint
Fritz	Out of order
Funny papers	Comics

G

Garage sale	Jumble sale
Garbage/trash	Rubbish
Garbage can	Dustbin
Garter belt	Suspender belt
Garters	Suspenders
Gas/gasoline	Petrol
Gas station	Petrol/filling station
Gear shift	Gear lever
German shepherd	Alsatian, police dog
Gidget	A bubbly, pretty girl
Gimp/gimpy	Cripple/lame
Gizmo	Mechanical tool - a what d' you call it
Glitch	A hitch, bug, failure in equipment/program
Glory hole	Spare room used for storage
Goof	To make an error

Goof ball	Eccentric
	Sleeping pill/ tranquilizer/narcotic
Goon	Thug
Goose bumps	Goose pimples
Gotten *(pp of 'to get')*	Got *I've gotten the baby's formula ready.*
Grab bag	Lucky dip
Grade	Form in school
Grade crossing	Level crossing
Grade school	Primary school
Granola	Muesli
Graveyard shift	Working all night
Green thumbs	Green fingers
Grip	Suitcase
Grippe	Influenza
Grits	Coarsely ground food: maize, wheat or rice
Ground meat	Minced meat
	(**ground round** is the best mince)
Ground wire	Earth wire/earth
Grubs	Dirty old jeans
Gulf States	American states on the Gulf of Mexico
Gumshoe	Detective (someone who walks quietly)
Gyp	Cheat, swindle

Haberdasher	Men's outfitter
Hairy	Dangerous
Hang in there	To complete a course, a task
Hard nosed	Tough, hard headed
Hardware store	Ironmonger's shop
Hash over	To talk over
Hat check girl	Cloakroom attendant
Hick	Small-town or an unsophiscated person
Hike	Boost
Hit	Murder, kill
Hockey	Ice hockey (**hockey** is field hockey)
Hog-tied	Tied up, powerless
Homemaker	Housewife
Hood	Car bonnet
	Gangster (**hoodlum**)
	Neighbourhood
Hoof and mouth disease	Foot and mouth disease
Hope chest	Bottom draw
Horn	Telephone
	Pommel of a saddle
Humidor	Cigar box
Humungous	Huge, very big

	Hunky-dory	Satisfactory, excellent
	Hurdy gurdy	Barrel organ
I	**Icebox**	Refrigerator
	Incorporated	Limited
	Information	Directory enquires (telephone)
	Installment plan	Hire purchase (note English spelling - instalment)
	Intermission	Interval
	Intern	Houseperson in a hospital or student working in a profession for little or no pay to gain work experience
	Inventory	Stock
J	**Jacklight**	Portable lantern
	Jam	Thick conserve with pieces of fruit in it (British jam is called jelly)
	Jammies	Pyjamas
	Janitor	Caretaker
	Jelly	Jam
	Jelly roll	Swiss roll
	Jerk	Slow-witted person
	Jimmy	Jemmy

John	Toilet
Juice	Influence, authority
Jump suit	One-piece garment/child's playsuit
Jump rope	Skipping rope

K

Kerosene	Paraffin
Key punch	Card punch
Kickback	Money paid illegally in a business deal
Kiss-off	Abrupt dismissal, often rude
Knee pants	Short trousers
Knickers	Plus-fours
Knock up	To make pregnant
Kook/kooky	Eccentric

L

Labor union	Trade union
Ladybug	Ladybird
Lard-ass/lard-bucket	Fat individual
Lawyer/attorney	Solicitor
Leatherneck	US Marine
Legal holiday	Bank holiday
Levee	Structure built on the side of a river to prevent flooding

Licence plate	Number plate
Life preserver	Life buoy
Lightening bug	Glow worm
Lima bean	Broad bean
Line-up	Queue
Line-up (in prison)	Identification parade
Liquor store	Off licence/wine merchant
Liverwurst	Liver sausage
Loaded	Rich, drunk
Lobby	Foyer
Locate	To settle in a home, to relocate
Loft	To raise or hoist
Loge	Front of the dress circle at a theatre
Log roll	To do a good turn in return for a favour
Long distance	Trunk call
Longshoreman	Docker who loads and unloads ships
Lost and found	Lost property
Lot	A piece of land
Lounge jacket	Smoking jacket
Love seat	Settee
Lox	Smoked salmon
Lumber room	Box room, store room

M

Maid of honor	Bridesmaid
Mail	Post
Mail drop	Letter box
Mailman	Postman
Make reservation	Book
Malted milk	Sweet, milk drink containing ice cream and malt
Market	To shop
Marquee	Illuminated sign
Math	Maths
Maverick	Cow that strays from the herd (person who leaves a group e.g. a political group)
Mean	Nasty (not necessarily stingy)
Meat grinder	Mincer
Median strip/divider	Central reservation (road)
Mezzanine/loge	Dress circle (cinema/theatre)
Mickey Mouse	Insignificant, trivial
Molasses	Black treacle
Momentarily	Very soon, in a moment (not for a moment)
Monkey wrench	Adjustable spanner
Mortician	Undertaker
Mother in law apartment	Granny flat
Motorman	Train or tram driver

Movie	Film
Moviehouse/theatre	Cinema
Muffler	Silencer on a car
Murphy bed	A bed which folds into a cupboard
Muss up	To make untidy, to mess up
Mutt	Mongrel dog
Mutual fund	Unit trust

N

Neckerchief	Tiny scarf
Nerd	Boring person
Newsboy	Newspaper boy
Newsdealer/news stand	Newsagent
Newsman	Journalist
Nickel	Five-cent coin
Night crawler	Worm used as fishing bait
Night school	Evening classes
Nightstick	Truncheon
Nipple (on a baby's bottle)	Teat
Nitty-gritty	The precise details, the basic facts
No go	Stop, unable to proceed
No no	Something that should never be done
Notions	Haberdashery

O

Odometer	Mileometer
Office (doctor's/dentist)	Surgery
Off the wall	Strange, unusual
Oilers	oilskins
Oleo	Margarine
One horse town	Small town
One way ticket	Single ticket
Orchestra seats	Front seats in a theatre, stalls
Out-house	Outdoor toilet
Outlet/socket (electric)	Point/powerpoint
Out to lunch	Crazy (the brain has stopped working and has taken a break)
Overalls	Dungarees/boiler suit
Overpass	Flyover

P

Pacifier	Baby's dummy
Pack rat	Hoarder
Pancake turner	Fish slice
Panhandler	Beggar
Pantie hose	Tights
Pants	Trousers
Paper	Money

Paraffin	Paraffin wax (**Paraffin** as used in Britain is **kerosene** in America.)
Parakeet	Budgerigar
Parka	Anorak
Parking lot	Car park
Parkway	Main thoroughfare, usually lined with trees
Parley	Conference
Parlor car	First-class railway carriage with individual seats
Pass	Overtake
Patrolman	Policeman
Patrol wagon	Black Maria
Pavement	Road
Pay dirt	Mineral rich soil e.g. discovered by a prospector
Pay station	Telephone call box
Peeler	Striptease dancer
Penitentiary	Prison
Period (punctuation)	Full stop
Person-to-person	Personal call
Phonograph	Record player
Pick-up truck	Open back lorry
Pinkie	Little finger
Pit (fruit)	Stone

Pitcher	Jug
Pizazz	Spark, vitality
Pony	Crib (for exams)
Pony up	To pay a debt
Pooch	Dog
Popsicle	Ice lolly on a stick
Pot holders/gloves	Oven gloves /cloth
Potato chips	Crisps
Pot roast	Meat dish cooked in a casserole
Powdered sugar/ confectioner's sugar	Icing sugar
Precinct	District
President (business)	Chairman
Private school	Public school/private school
Produce	Greengroceries (fruit and vegetables)
Prom	School/university dance (from promenade)
Prowl car	Police patrol car
Public school	State school
Pull-off	Lay-by
Purse/pocket book	Handbag (a purse as in Britain is a **change purse** in America)
Pushcart	Wheelbarrow

Q

Quarter	25-cent coin
Quarterback	Important position in American football
Quirt	Riding whip

R

Raft	Large amount
Railroad	Railway (to force)
Raincheck	Postponement
Raise	Rise - pay rise
Raisin	Sultana
Raisin bread	Currant bread
Realtor/real estate agent	Estate agent
Rear view mirror	Wing mirror
Recess	Break (e.g. between classes)
Redcap	Railway porter
Redneck	Ignorant person
Rest room	Toilet/cloakroom
Résumé	Curriculum vitae
Revenue officer	Official who upholds the law against the illegal production of alcohol
Review	Revise e.g. for exams
Rhinestone	Diamanté
Ride	Harass, tease

Ringer	Look-alike
Rinky-dink	Inexpensive, cheap
Roller coaster	Big dipper
Rookie	Novice
Roomer	Lodger
Root beer	A soft, non-alcoholic drink
Round trip ticket	Return ticket
Rubber	Condom
Rummage sale	Jumble sale

S

Sack	Bed
Sack lunch	Packed lunch
Sales clerk/girl	Shop assistant
Saltine	Salted cracker usually served with soup
Sandbag	Sack filled with sand and used as a cudgel
	To knock someone over with a blow from behind
Sand box	Sand pit
Sap	Cosh
Sashay	To walk stylishly for effect
Sass	To give cheek, impudence
Scanties	Panties, underclothes
Schedule	Timetable

Schmaltz	Chicken fat
	Too much sentimentality
Schmuch	Stupid and usually nasty
Schnook	Fool
Scratch pad	Scribbling notepad
Screen door	Outer door of mosquito mesh
Scuttlebutt	Gossip, rumour
Second floor	First floor
Second guess	Be wise after something has happened
Sedan	Saloon car
Seltzer	Soda water
Semester (school two in a year)	Term (three in a year)
Set	Lay (a table)
Sewer pipe/soil pipe	Drain (indoor)
Shade	Window blind or awning
Shades	Sunglasses
Shebang	All, everything
	Party
Sheers/underdrapes	Net curtains
Sherbet	Ice/sorbet
Shoestring	Shoelace/bootlace

Shorts	Underpants as well as short trousers
Shredded (coconut)	Desiccated coconut
Sideburns	Sideboards
Sidewalk	Pavement
Silverware	Cutlery
Skillet	Frying pan
Slammer	Jail
Sneakers	Gym shoes/plimsolls
Snuck	To sneak
Soda cracker	Cream cracker
Softball	Game like baseball played with a softer, larger ball
Speed way	Motorway
Speed zone (cars)	Restricted speed area
Spike heels	Stiletto heels
Standing	Parking (used on road signs)
Station	Extension on a telephone
Straight up	Neat, no water (in a drink)
Streetcar	Tram
Stroller	Infant's pushchair
Sub-division	Housing estate
Superhighway	Motorway
Suspenders	Braces

T

Tab	Bill
Table cream	Single cream
Tag	Label
Tea kettle	Kettle
Teed off	Fed up
Tennies	Tennis shoes/plimsolls
Texas gate	Cattle grid
Thanksgiving	US national holiday (4th Thursday in November)
Threads	Clothes
Thumb tack/tack	Drawing pin
Tic-tac-toe	Noughts and crosses
Ticked off	Browned off, fed up
Top (car)	Roof/hood
Tracking	Selection by ability e.g. streaming in schools
Trade	Swap
Traffic circle	Round-about
Trailer park	Caravan site
Trash	Rubbish
Truck stop	Transport café
Trunk (car)	Boot
Tuxedo	Dinner suit/dinner jacket
Twister	Tornado

U

Undershirt	Vest
Unglued	Mad
Upgrade	Uphill
	Improving
Upset price	Reserve price
Uptown	Residential area away from the city centre

V

Vacationer	Holiday-maker
Vacuum bottle flask	Thermos flask
Vamoose	Scram, vanish
Vest	Waistcoat
Visiting fireman	Someone from out of town come to see the sights

W

Waitlist, to	Put on a waiting list
Walking papers	To be dismissed, the sack
Wash cloth	Flannel for washing oneself
Wash up	To wash oneself - not dishes
Water heater (electric)	Immersion heater
Water heater (gas)	Geyser
Wax paper	Greaseproof paper
Wedding band	Wedding ring

Wet-back	Illegal immigrant
Wharf/pier	Quay
Whistlestop town	Small town - train only stops when whistle is blown
Wholewheat	Wholemeal
Windbreaker	Windcheater
Windshield	Windscreen
Wire	Telegram
Wrangler	Cowboy who breaks in wild horses
Wrap	Coat

Y

Yard	Garden
Yardbird	Convict
Yard man	Gardener
Yo-yo	Stupid or crazy person

Z

Za (abbrev.)	Pizza
Zap	Knock down, kill
Zee	Z
Zinger	Bullseye
Zip code	Post code
Zipper	Zip

ENGLISH - AMERICAN

English	American
Achiever	Comer
All dressed up	Duded up
American footballer	Quarterback
Anger	Dander
Angry	To go ape
Ankle sock	Bobby sox
Annoy	To bug
Anorak	Parka
Appointment book	Date book
Apprentice waiter	Bus boy
Articulated lorry	Trailer truck
Aubergine	Eggplant
Autumn	Fall
Avocado	Alligator pear
Baby food	Formula
Baby's dummy	Pacifier
Baking tray	Cookie sheet
Bank account	Checking account
Bank holiday	Legal holiday
Bank note	Bill
Barman	Bar keep
Barrel organ	Hurdy gurdy
Bath (to)	Bathing (not swimming)
Beach hut	Cabana
Bed	Sack
Bed (folding)	Murphy bed
Beggar	Pan handler
Bespoke	Custom made
Big (very)	Humungous
Big dipper	Roller coaster
Bill	Tab
Bill (food)	Check
Biscuit (sweet)	Cookie
Biscuit (unsweetened)	Cracker
Black Maria	Patrol wagon
Black treacle	Molasses
Block of flats	Apartment building
Bonnet (car)	Hood
Book (reserve)	Make a reservation
Boost	Hike
Boot (car)	Trunk
Bootlace	Shoestring

Bottom/bum	Butt	**Carry cot**	Baby buggy
Bottom draw	Hope chest	**Caravan site**	Trailer park
Bowler hat	Derby	**Casserole (meat)**	Pot roast
Box room	Lumber room	**Cattle grid**	Texas gate
Braces	Suspenders	**Centenary**	Centennial
Breasts	Bazoom	**Central reservation**	
Bridesmaid	Maid of honor	**(road)**	Median, strip, divider
Broad bean	Lima bean	**Chairman**	
Broken	On the blink	**(business)**	President
Browned off, fed up	Ticked off	**Cheap**	Chintzy, rinky dink,
Budgerigar	Parakeet		penny ante
Burglary (by police/		**Cheat**	Gyp
officials)	Bag job	**Cheesed off**	Teed off
Bullseye	Zinger	**Chemist**	Druggist
		Chemist's shop	Drugstore, pharmacy
Cake (fluffy)	Angel cake	**Cheque**	Check
Cake (small)	Biscuit, cruller	**Chest of drawers**	Bureau, dresser
Camp bed	Cot	**Chips**	French fried potatoes
Candy floss	Cotton candy	**Cigar box**	Humidor
Car park	Parking lot	**Cigarette**	Butt
Cards (pack)	Deck	**Cinema**	Movie house/theatre
Caretaker	Janitor	**City centre**	Down town

Class/form	Grade	**Cream cracker**	Soda cracker
Cloakroom	Check room	**Crib (exams)**	Pony
Cloakroom		**Cripple**	gimp
attendant	Hat check girl	**Crisps**	Potato chips
Clothes	Threads	**Cupboard**	Closet
Clothes peg	Clothes pin	**Currant bread**	Raisin bread
Clout	Juice	**Curriculum vitae**	Résumé
Coat	Wrap	**Curtains (net)**	Sheers, underdrapes
Collector for an illegal		**Curtains (opaque)**	Drapes
organisation	Bag man	**Cutlery**	Silverware
Comicxs	Funny papers		
Condom	Rubber	**Daily record**	Blotter
Conference	Parley	**Dance (school,**	
Conscription	Draft	university)	Prom
Conserve	Jam	**Dangerous**	Hairy
Convict	Yardbird	**Death duties**	Estate tax
Convoy	Caravan	**Debt (to pay)**	Pony up
Cornflour	Cornstarch	**Desiccated coconut**	Shredded coconut
Cotton wool	Cotton	**Desk diary**	Date book
Cow that strays	Maverick	**Detective**	Dick, gumshoe
Cravat	Ascot	**Diamanté**	Rhinestone
Crazy	Out to lunch, unglued		

Directory enquiries (telephone)	Information
Dishpan	Washing up bowl
Dismissal (often rude/abrupt)	Kiss off
District	Precinct
Docker	Longshoreman
Dog	Pooch
Dollar	Buck
Door made of mesh	Screen door
Drain (indoors)	Sewer
Draper	Dry goods store
Draughts	Checkers
Drawing pin	Thumb tack
Dress circle	Mezzanine, loge
Dressing gown	Bathrobe
Drunk	Loaded
Dual carriageway	Divided highway
Dungarees	Overalls
Dust bin	Ash, garbage, trash can
Earth (wire)	Ground wire
Eccentric	Goof ball, kook, kooky, off the wall
Egg flip	Eggnog
Eiderdown	Comforter
Electric point	Outlet
Error	Blooper
Estate agent	Realtor
Europe	Yarrup
Evening classes	Night school
Evening shirt	Boiled shirt
Everything	Shebang
Excellent	Dandy
Excited	To go ape
Extension (telephone)	Station
Facts (basic)	Nitty gritty
Failure	Bummer
Farewell	Kiss off
Fat person	Lard ass, lard bucket
Favour (to do)	Log roll
Field hockey	Hockey

English	American
Film	Movie
Fine	Dandy
Fire hydrant	Fire plug
Firework	Firecracker
First floor	Ground floor
Fish slice	Pancake turner
Five cent coin	Nickel
Flannel	Wash cloth
Flat	Apartment
Flat (owner occupied)	Condominium, condo
Flatterer	Apple polisher
Floor	Deck
Flyerover	Overpass
Foot and mouth disease	Hoof and mouth disease
Forbid	Enjoin
Forbidden	No, no
Form/class	Grade
Fourth Thursday in November	Thanksgiving
Foyer	Lobby
Frying pan	Skillet
Full stop	Period (punctuation)
Funny bone	Crazy bone
Gangster	Hood
Gardener	Yard man
Geyser	Water heater (gas)
Glow worm	Lightening bug
Good	Dandy, humungous
Good order (in)	Apple pie order
Goods wagon	Freight car
Goose pimples	Goose bumps
Gossip	Scuttlebutt
Got	Gotten
Greaseproof paper	Wax paper
Green fingers	Green thumb
Grill	Broil
Ground floor	First floor
Guard	Conductor
Guard (on a train)	Brakeman
Gun dog	Bird dog
Guttering	Eavestrough

Gymkhana	Horse show
Haberdashery	Notions
Hairgrip, hair pin	Bobby pin
Handbag	Purse, pocket book
Harass (tease)	Ride
Hard hat	Bowler
Hat (small, woollen)	Toque
High, elation	Buzz
Hire purchase	Installment plan
Hitch (failure)	Glitch
Hockey	Field hockey
Hoist (to)	Loft
Holiday	Vacation
Homeless woman	Bag lady
Homework	Assignment
Hotel rate	American plan
Housewife	Homemaker
Housing estate	Sub-division
Ice (water/sorbet)	Sherbet
Ice hockey	Hockey

Ice lolly	Popsicle
Icing sugar	Confectionery sugar
	Powdered sugar
Identification parade	Line up
Ignorant person	Redneck
Illegal immigrant	Wet-back
Illuminated sign	Marquee
Immersion heater	Water heater (electric)
Improve	Upgrade
Impudence	Sass
Infant's pushchair	Stroller
Influence	Juice
Influence of drugs/ alcohol	Buzz
Influenza	Gripe
Insecticide spray	Aerosol bomb
Interval	Intermission
Ironmonger's	Hardware store
Jail	Slammer
Jam	Jelly

Jeans (dirty/old)	Grubs	**Level crossing**	Grade crossing
Jittery	Antsy	**Life jacket**	Life preserver
Journalist	Newsman/woman	**Lift**	Elevator
Jug	Pitcher	**Limited (company)**	Incorporated (Inc)
Jumble sale	Garage sale	**Liver sausage**	Liverwurst
	Rummage sale	**Lodger**	Roomer
		Look alike	Ringer
Kettle	Tea kettle	**Lorry (open-back)**	Pick up truck
Kill	Hit, zap	**Lost and found**	Lost property
Kiosk	Booth	**Lot (everything)**	Shebang
Knock down	Zap	**Lucky dip**	Grab bag
		Lunch (packed)	Sack lunch
Label	Tag		
Ladybird	Lady bug	**Mad**	Unglued
Lame	Gimpy	**Maize**	Corn, grits (grains)
Lantern (portable)	Jacklight	**Mate**	Buddy
Large amount	Raft	**Maths**	Math
Lay (a table)	Set	**Megaphone**	Bullhorn
Lay by	Pull off	**Men's outfitter**	Haberdasher
Leader (orchestra)	Concert master	**Minced (meat)**	Ground meat
Left luggage office	Checkroom	**(Best meat)**	Ground round
Leggings (leather)	Chaps	**Mincer**	Meat grinder

English	American
Mistake	Blooper, goof
Money paid illicitly in a deal	Kick-back
Mongrel (dog)	Mutt
Motorway	Expressway, freeway, speedway, superhighway
Mudguard (car)	Fender
Murder	Hit
Nappy	Diaper
Nasty	Mean
Newsagent	Newsdealer, news stand
Newspaper	Newsboy
Newspaper leading article	Editorial
Night shift	Graveyard shift
No water (drinks)	Neat, straight up
Non-alcoholic drink	Root beer
Nothing	Zilch
Noughts and crosses	Tic-tac-toe
Number plate	Licence plate
Off licence	Liquor store
Oilskins	Oilers
Open air stands in a sports stadium	Bleachers
Oven gloves	Pot holders
Pageboy (hotel)	Bellhop
Pal	Buddy
Pancake	Flapjack
Panties	Scanties
Paraffin	Kerosene
Paraffin wax	Paraffin
Parcel	Package
Parking	Standing
Party	Shebang
Patience	Solitaire
Paunch	Bay window
Pavement	Sidewalk
Pelmet	Valance
Persevere	Hang in there

Persuade	Buffalo	**a group**	Maverick
Petrol	Gas, gasoline	**Personal call**	Person to person
Petrol station	Filling station	**Primary school**	Grade school
Phone in	Call in	**Prison**	Penitentiary
Piece of land	Lot	**Professional student**	
Pillar box	Mail box, mail drop	**working to gain**	
Playsuit (child's)	Jump suit	**experience**	Intern
Plimsolls	Deck shoes, sneakers	**Public school**	Private school
Plus fours	Knickers	**Puritanical laws**	
Police dog	German shepherd dog	**on alcohol ...**	Blue laws
Policeman	Patrolman	**Pyjamas**	Jammies
Police patrol car	Prowl car		
Porter	Bellhop	**Quay**	Wharf, pier
Post	Mail	**Queue**	Line up
Postal code	Zip code	**Quilt**	Comforter
Postman	Mailman		
Postponement	Raincheck	**Railway**	Railroad
Pouffe	Hassock	**Railway porter**	Redcap
Pram	Baby buggy	**Receptionist**	Desk clerk
Pregnant (to make)	Knock up	**Recruit (new)**	Rookie
Preserve (food)	Can	**Refrigerator**	Ice box
Person who leaves		**Reprimand (to)**	Bawl out

Reserve, extra	Backlog	**Sack (dismiss)**	Can
Reserve price			Walking papers
(auction)	Upset price	**Sailor in US Navy**	Bluey jacket
Residential area away		**Saloon car**	Sedan
from city centre	Uptown	**Salt beef**	Corned beef
Restaurant (cheap)	Diner	**Salted cracker**	Saltine
Restricted speed		**Sandpit**	Sand box
area	Speed zone	**Satisfactory**	Hunky dory
Reversing light	Back up light (car)	**Scarf (small)**	Neckerchief
Revise for exams	Review	**Scone (cake)**	Biscuit
Rich	Loaded	**Scram**	Vamoose
Ridiculous	Cockamanny	**Scribbling pad**	Scratch pad
Riding whip	Quirt	**Season ticket**	Commuter ticket
Ring doughnut	Cruller	**Second-hand**	Pre-owned
Rise (pay)	Raise	**See**	Eyeball
River embankment	Levee	**Self catering**	Cook in
Road	Pavement	**Semi detached**	Duplex
Roof (car)	Hood, top	**Sentimentality**	Schmaltz
Roundabout	Traffic circle	**Service flats**	Apartment hotel
Rubber	Condom	**Settee**	Couch/sofa/love seat
Rubbish	Garbage, trash	**Settle in an area**	Locate
Rumour	Scuttlebutt	**Shoelace**	Shoestring

Shop (to)	Market	**Spare room**	Glory hole
Shop assistant	Sales clerk/person	**Speak badly of**	Bad mouth
Shopping trolley	Shopping cart	**Stake**	Ante
Short trousers	Knee pants	**Stalls**	Orchestra seats
Shut off	Can	**State school**	Public school
Sideboard	Sideburns	**States on Gulf of**	
Silencer (car)	Muffler	**Mexico**	Gulf States
Silo (grain)	Elevator	**Sticking plaster**	Adhesive tape
Single cream	Table cream	**Stiletto heels**	Spike heels
Skipping rope	Jump rope	**Stock**	Inventory
Skirting board	Baseboard	**Stone (fruit)**	Pit
Smoked salmon	Lox	**Stop**	No go
Smoking jacket	Lounge jacket	**Streaming in**	
Sneak (to)	Snuck	**schools**	Tracking
Soda water	Seltzer, club soda	**Striptease dancer**	Peeler
Sofa	Davenport	**Stupid person**	Schmuch, yo-yo
Soil containing minerals		**Stupid, nasty**	
(prospector's)	Pay dirt	**person**	Jerk
Solicitor	Lawyer, attorney	**Sub-editor**	Copy reader
Soon	Momentarily	**Suit (one-piece)**	Jump suit
Sorbet	Sherbet	**Suit cases**	Bags, grips
Spanner	Wrench	**Sultana**	Raisin

Sunglasses	Shades	**Theatrical touring**	Barnstorm
Superior	Crackerjack	**Thermos flask**	Vacuum flask
Surgery	Doctor's/dentist's office	**Thoroughfare**	Parkway
Suspenders	Braces	**Thug**	Goon
Swap	Trade	**Ticket (free)**	Annie Oakley
Sweets	Candy	**Ticket (single)**	One way ticket
Swindle	Gyp	**Ticket (return)**	Round trip ticket
Swiss roll	Jelly roll	**Tied up**	Hog-tied
		Tights	Panty hose
Talk over	Hash over	**Timetable**	Schedule
Tap	Faucet	**Toilet (indoor)**	John, rest room
Tea trolley	Tea cart	**Toilet (outdoor)**	Out-house
Tease	Ride	**Tool**	Gizmo
Teat	Nipple	**Torch**	Flashlight
Telephone	Horn	**Tornado**	Twister
Telephone call	Buzz	**Town (small)**	Whistle stop,
Telephone call box	Pay station		one horse town
Television	Boob tube	**Trade union**	Labour union
Temper	Dandy	**Traffic roundabout**	Traffic circle
Tennis shoes	Tennies	**Training camp**	
Term (school - 3)	Semester (s)	**(military)**	Boot camp
Textiles	Dry goods	**Tram**	Street car

English	American
Transport café	Truck stop
Travel at speed	Barrel
Trivial	Mickey Mouse
Trousers	Pants
Truncheon	Billy club, nightstick
Trunk call	Long distance
Turn ups (trousers)	Cuffs
Uncovered stands in a stadium	Bleachers
Underpants	Shorts
Undertaker	Mortician
Unpaved road	Dirt road
Unsophisticated person	Hick
Useless	Bummer
U S Marine	Leatherneck
Untidy (to make)	Muss up
Vague	Acey deucy
Valuer	Appraiser
Vest	Undershirt
V I P address book	Bluebook
Vitality	Pizazz
Waistcoat	Vest
Walk with style	Sashay
Wallet	Billfold/notecase
Wardrobe	Closet
Wash oneself	Wash up
Wedding ring	Wedding band
Wet paint	Fresh paint
Wheelbarrow	Pushcart
Wholemeal	Wholewheat
Windcheater	Windbreaker
Window blind	Shade
Windscreen	Windshield
Wine merchant	Liquor store
Wing (car)	Fender
Wing mirror	Rear view mirror
Wise after the event	Second guess
Woman	Broad